Bateman and Goto's coll
nostalgic creative autobi
their relationship to their fathers, their lives, and
through the transfiguring effects of alcohol, the narrative
travels from glamorous nightclubs and the Jade Market
in Taipei to Peterborough, Ontario and Nanton, Alberta.
Through memory, mourning, geographies and sexualities, this
poetic narrative is at once a memento mori and meditations
upon wabi sabi.

also by David Bateman

Invisible Foreground
Impersonating Flowers
Salad Days
What Dreadful Things to Say about Someone
    Who has just Paid for my Lunch

also by Hiromi Goto

Chorus of Mushrooms
The Kappa Child
The Water of Possibility
Hopeful Monsters
Half World

wait until late afternoon
or *distilled, decanted & debauched*

a collaborative long poem by
david bateman
&
hiromi goto

Frontenac House
Calgary, Alberta

Copyright © 2009 by David Bateman and Hiromi Goto

All rights reserved, including moral rights. No part of this publication may be reproduced or transmitted in any form or by any means electronic or mechanical including recording, photocopying, or any information storage retrieval system without permission in writing from the author or publisher or ACCESS copyright, except by a reviewer or academic who may quote brief passages in a review or critical study.

Book and cover design: Epix Design
Cover Image: Hiromi Goto and Neil Petrunia
Author photo: Unidentified waitress

Library and Archives Canada Cataloguing in Publication

Bateman, David
 Wait until late afternoon, or Distilled, decanted & debauched : a collaborative long poem / David Bateman, Hiromi Goto.

ISBN 978-1-897181-30-0

 I. Goto, Hiromi, 1966- II. Title.
III. Title: Distilled, decanted & debauched.

PS8553.A8254W35 2009   C811'.54   C2009-903168-X

We acknowledge the support of the Canada Council for the Arts for our publishing program. We also acknowledge the support of The Alberta Foundation for the Arts.

 Canada Council   Conseil des Arts
for the Arts   du Canada

Printed and bound in Canada
Published by Frontenac House Ltd.
1138 Frontenac Avenue S.W.
Calgary, Alberta, T2T 1B6, Canada
Tel: 403-245-2491 Fax: 403-245-2380
editor@frontenachouse.com www.frontenachouse.com

I thank god for the small but beautiful way
in which alcohol has touched our lives today
                      David Bateman

For me and David
                      Hiromi Goto

acknowledgements

Betty Marjorie Wyatt, Harry Vernon Bateman, Weldon Joseph Kennedy, and all of the other fabulous co-dependents who have passed through my life, and the grand and gracious hosting of Ashok Mathur, who continues to bless my daze with the presence and the pleasure of larger than life liquor cabinets from coast to shining coast. D.B.

I gratefully acknowledge everyone with whom I've shared a drink. I am also extremely grateful to the Simon Fraser University Writer-in-Residence Program and Canada Council. I didn't spend any of the grant money on booze... H.G

wait until late afternoon

H   one

she forgot to
take aspirin the night
before with two tall
glasses of water

crept outdoors
in time to catch
the anal pucker
of spent morning
glories in the afternoon

D two

he remembered tylenol
advil, acetaminaphin
sinus relief tablets
when medicine cabinets
like wall hung brooks, streams, waterfalls
sparsely fed by clear
syringe like rays of hangover remedies

wading through capsules
tablets, caffeine clouds
peonies in the dank tall fog
of mornings after
glamorous spent evenings
sipping, gulping, gullet dancing
into paradise

H three

every friday night she confronted
and accepted that she was straight

gin, Bombay

       okay she liked it
dirty probably
    that first time
                    she was loose
enough to speak
she said, i've admired you from afar
and felt
affinity   the way
               you held yourself
in public spaces

how your father
was an alcoholic

like mine

D four

his daddy waltzed through
bar room brawls with himself
fighting shadows of former glory
bumping into logs, overturned chairs, tables
faintly masochistic forms
at the Ship 'n Shore hotel

furniture funnelling dignity
out of mid-century madness
in the trenches of Northern Europe
burying army jeeps for farmers to refurbish

this was god 'n country
home to roost and raise a family
among remains of rotting reliquaries
vessels of unsung love

sons and daughters born
lifted into some toughened
frail fey masculinity of fear
and then he meets her

across so many crowded rooms
her dignity, like his
seems shrouded in the sheer glamour
of unadulterated muffled cries

"make mine dirty" becoming the common call
of a wounded soldier's loins

H   five

your father started drinking
                                        the night
  you were born,
  her mother said
              when she was still
                             horrified
                      enough to feel
the blame

not knowing
it hadn't been placed
                   just a marker
                                    between upright
       and sober
           to the nightly
slaughter Promethean
torment for an evening's
respite and in god's house
every sunday
                      the sweet
     cologne of rye and sweat
what's your poison, hey
you drink like i do
she said drunk
but not so she couldn't see
                            something familiar

D   six

        Her

copious amounts of Bombay gin
a generous dash of pomegranate juice
shaken on ice, not stirred

sliced halves of purple figs
revealing luscious pink interiors
tantalizing curl of lemon rind
swirling like thirst-quenching flesh
to parched nomadic lips
along the edge of one martini glass

pour   nirvana

to   His

satin pillows on the kitchen floor
legs crossed as small refrigerator bulbs
illuminate full frontal boozing
at 2 a.m.

coming honestly to memories
of his mama's forays into
happy freezer-side hours

one chilling bottle
one straw
one comfort cushion
furnishing habitual havens with
mandarin infused   Xanadu

sip   'til you flip

H   seven

a regimen
of libation
                        a phalanx of empty bottles
                        those nights

euthanized the days
awash with the chirrup of sparrows
                        echoing in the reeking rafters
                        her oto-san
enfolded in a past
tense narrative
                    and a daughter to unfold her
present

raising a family
                        with the dead

she liked how he would
                        drink
anything, he wasn't
an alcohol snob they
shared a similar
                backyard childhood
aspiring flowerbeds and hedges
                  a martini up the social ladder
(be careful)
they were both so
                            quiet
their fathers were taking
a little nap

D   eight

having seen

the way he held himself
in public spaces
how his father
was an alcoholic
like hers

beneath an elegant demeanour
fragile layers of dignity
peel away as ounces of alcohol
release the repetitive glow
of ice cubes rattling
through crystal tumblers
drenched in Grey Goose
freshly frozen blueberries
vibrant green plastic geckos
swimming into some tequila horizon
party favours released by over-zealous hostesses

he holds himself – aloof – and falling

into

(ounces and ounces of)

induced
camaraderie

shy, inflected

love

H   nine

tincture

a soft infusion
like the first long draw
from a dirty
martini after the exhaust
of the day
the jaws loosen at
the hips
the eyes mellow warm
glow rising from the belly

warm

after her hand
drops on his arm a gesture
turns into a touch
can i
get you
another
she asks

the face's sudden burn
for no reason
at all

D   ten

into the fray   ragged beverage edges
                            watermelon infusions
vodka vindictive   verification   all is
    swelling

dilation of cerebral arteries
muscle tightness   decreased
anti-diuretic hormones   (ADH)

rising blood alcohol level
kidneys excreting water
alcohol-induced dehydration

ADH levels rise   urinary output
decreases   one thirsty puppy

hangover into full swing puffy eyes
                         fluid retention
                         (aka edema)

a pathology of pomp and ceremony
one heraldic headache   family symbols   coats of
arms

                          legs akimbo
sweaty sheets damp   crumpled
knotted into limbs

clinical and familial details fade into one final
retreat into mythic remedies
"hair of the dog" prolonging an inevitable
swing out of inebriative aftermath

facing folkloric music
he remembers a doctor's words:
    if both parents were alcoholics
    you have an eighty-five percent chance of
    becoming one yourself

belated thank-you notes
scribbled on coasters and posted on swizzle sticks
tiny makeshift signs planted
flags of forefathers

staggering into the dubious generosity of
genetic re-birth

    thanks mom and dad
    you did all the work

with only fifteen percent of the labour left
forearms rising
fists clutching tumblers
toasting heritage

    the rest is

                past

H eleven

shunning diurnal consumption
oh holy night
        where cups runneth over
                                                  cars
  swerving in
                    and out
                        of the centre
                    line a blur
                      of yellow staggers
                swagger
                            ing
                      the blue line
                turning a
                        sobriety test
          into a funny family

story, the joke's on us

it helps me sleep
i like the taste
it's relaxing
it takes away the edge
i only drink socially

trips
    the tongue curling

catch
    the last drop

watch
    you don't become

what you abhor

    what you

                love

D twelve

vicarious denial
better living through chemistry
yeast fermentation
believing we consume
in liquid form
mostly grains and fruits
mashing carbohydrate-rich material
fermenting for a regulated time
tends to toxicity with complex chemistry
ethanol additive   makes high life lighter
only water-clear vodkas
remain relatively free
of chemical mix

relative freedom

just another way to say
no brain cells left to lose

bring on the waterless booze

let's have a ball   if that's all

                          there is

H   thirteen

how often do you
drink she asked him her legs crossed
one arm extended past
her knee her empty
glass nonchalant
                       ly in her loose
grip
     oh, every day with my
soap, he quipped,
seriously casual the causal
effects of a prolonged childhood
exposure
     he went to the kitchen
the staccato clatter
icy metal shaker beading cold
enough to burn
     i've decided if i'm going to drink
she called across the room
i'll drink high quality booze!
     it's gotta be better for you,
she muttered averting
                              her thirst

to the night window
the silhouette of the city
turning into lights

D   fourteen

"an unbearable lightness"

>   he whispered
>   welling up

citing authors he could never remember

is it early onset dementia
or simply mental blocks born of trauma
overexposure to classic worldly narratives
of word weary drinkers

before he learned to read

his first formula
rum and coke
a taste of working class paradise

inaugural sips at daddy's knee

blossoming into florid first kiss
alliterative praxis
wordsmiths wrought with lyric longing

he travelled to Taipei City
reading tours wrenched by individualists

she was with him   bars filled with   young men

a hint of make-up   theirs   hers

the butch-femmery of gender distillation
fermenting identity into

"legs crossed
one arm extended past
her knee

her empty
glass nonchalant
             ly in her loose grip"

looking lovingly through so many faces
he dreams of a family long since buried
in the muck of mortality

eyes a bevy of beautiful young men
second only to the taut crafted confidence
the resounding physical beauty and array of
her presence in this
colonized wanton wonderland

he quips

    we have crossed
    international   date lines
    together turning daylight
    into darkness

    we have taken friendship
    across   borders
    into bidden territories

    and come out alive

    kicking

his family of friends, and the   glamour of

televised alcoholism

the only blood lines he can bear to witness

    laced with familiar distress
    comforts him in a variety of time zones

    watching their cries
    hearing them reaching out

    he'll be damned
    by toasting them
    with glasses of lurid leftover zinfandel

    legs crossed   one arm   ex ten ded
               non cha lant ly

    craving cooking claret by the sink
    at eight a.m.
    in his robe and argyle socks

    awaiting mid-mourning instalments
    of his favourite soap

    wherever he hangs his hat then wanders

        determined blithely
        to enjoy a panoply
        of global insobriety

                        come hither Pucks

                        wine filled sprites
"be drunken"   always

taste the   summer of your   lives

                        mid-mornings
evenings
                        afternoons

            knowing

somewhere
                        in this world

it is

                        happy hour

H   fifteen

(the nice thing
about booze
is how trauma

                        can spin
into pleasure)

                  tora uma, her mother said
                  too much
                  can cause irreparable
                  damage
                  tora uma, her daughter
                  puzzled,
        Tiger horse
                  how can tiger horse
                  cause so much
                  damage? her father
born
                  a Tiger she
a horse…
                  tora uma, her mother
                  said, tora uma!

        It's English!

when understanding

                  parted
the tiger's mauling   of the noble equus,

she began laughing
so hard she
peed

                        (the tendency
                        to loop back
                        a gin spin
                        on a sad story)

a grin
spinning the table
Lazy Susan playing
Russian roulette
                        (a maudlin trait)
blame flies
with centrifugal force
                                        blunt
                        trauma
to the childish heart

again

she didn't know why
she switched
            to bloody marys
on the plane

self-conscious
                        retching
long into the morning
hoping he could sleep
                through her wretched
            knowing
he's no stranger
to the porcelain
pillow

a grin
        flecks of vomit
bitter on her tongue
       how
  sweet

the water

                              after

her first time
in Vegas

D   sixteen

Las Vegas
        Taipei City

Nicosia   Yaletown   False Creek

Omemee   Vancouver Island

indoor snowy slopes in   Dubai

the sheer poetic phantasmatic desire
to set one's self on fire
and travel down those
deceptive pro-plebeian plasticized alps
in the midst of site specific mayhem

trauma travels well
meeting in these glamorous places
orange Absolut compliments of casino bar boys

keys, deserts, islands in the sand, lime martinis
2 parts Malibu Mudslide laced with Coconut Rum
2 parts Stoli Milli Vanilli Vodka
1 part lime juice
shake all ingredients with ice
in cocktail shaker
strain into martini glass

sing   a   long

continue to converse
cursing the wasteful mindless morning practice
of fruit juice without vodka

drinking Baileys before bedtime
honouring dairy-based fluids
above all else
how his grandfather drank rum and milk
for his ulcer
keeled over in a department store dressing room
with a summer hat perched on his mottled brow god love
him
                        I tried to

died   mid-seventies
of a stroke   too much rye
                not enough coke

he met her suave gesticulative father
at a poetry reading
spectacular compact physique
gorgeous greying into icy winters
reminds him of her powerful elegant nuance
robust and petite
the trauma of bodied others
discovering through recovery
the "tora uma" of lifetimes spent un-frugally by
mocking malcontents
white pigeon-livered squawking creatures
blanched penile two-legged hogs
flying into dirt and dust

fleshy wan islands of skin
breaking into limbs and particles
of un-used brain cells

these are the boozy uncut cock tales

loving every blousy minute of their
dirty gin-rinsed lives

tiger-tini
mix one part orange crush
with fruit medley
two parts Grey Goose
shake, stir
raise glass   tilt   part lips

"durst not"   "taking in the bad air"
                    sip

      honour thy father

cry

H seventeen

the politics of alcohol
                colonialism the intricate
layers of implication
    oh how
to tell the Taiwanese bar
                       tender how
to make a dirty martini?
Japanese
Canadian in a
Japanese
Italian restaurant
                Taipei not so
   long
ago "returned"
to China, colonizers
bye bye
buy me a drink
and make it dirty
           it's oh so complicated
                   (complicit)
none of it
is clean
                                  any
                         way

gin, she said
lots of gin and some
brine from the olives
                make it salty
the waitress' well-
modulated
                       look

       he could not bear it
oh, i'll go tell them
he exclaimed
                swiftly
    chasing after her
                    martini saviour
      savour

    "these are the boozy uncut cock tales"

a fey white Canadian man behind
the counter
                mixing

contradictions and identitinis

she loved
that very moment

him

traversing continents
and histories
             their apparent
dis
    similar

heritage something poured
into a tall glass
                "drink me"

D   eighteen

to drink someone   in

                to taste

be   merry

these are the sad, gay, wild, long journeys into quiet
convolutions of night   caps

wearing many   hats

snuggling into rum-soaked fatherly fedoras

gownless   ball   caps

porkpie passages into millinery heaven

fearing for the bald doggerel inflected jargon of latent lyricism

but needing it so badly

soothing fact with fancy

before they met he went to Sicily   lisp in   tow

with unaccustomed friends

how does feyness and its fraught accoutrements translate into other bodied languages?

an exhausting day of backpacking
Eurail passes   made   in cramped
      compartments

the approaching brow of borrowed
French chapeaux
as he approaches a handsome Italian man
by the docks   of a bay
       and says, in sleepy dulcet tones,

lispily

              "which boat to Thithily"

wide Neapolitan smile, lips like ice cream
waiting   to be tasted
he eyes this femme white boy   toy

suppressing laughter   shrugging

          "ho una mancanza di inglese"

     Neapolitini

     1 ounce chocolate-infused vodka
     1 ounce Van Gogh coffee-flavoured vodka
     frozen fresh cherries
     cinnamon stick

          sprinkle with   blanched   white
               vanilla   fley-   verred
          shavings   from
          the bark   of some

          un-invented   tree

     garnish with tiny American flag

                        remove hat

    saluto

      stir   shake

      kiss

              sigh

H   nineteen

following more
care
      fully her father's path
        it took

close to two decades
                      to grow
comfortable drinking
    by
      herself

"soothing fact with fancy"
a high ball
                    tossed
back at five
on fridays
      was a modifier
not a past
        tense verb
    or noun

(surely her live/r would last a little longer
                    than her father's) the little tales
    decanted
before
      the first hit

she came out
                to her father
in Zimbabwe
      of course

    they had been drinking
    the floor's slight
        sloping
                where it reached
the walls'
       slight steeple
  toward the ceiling
              a pleasing
  slow spin
            resolving prejudice and blame

perfect timing
    between dessert
    and the decisive drink that splits

acceptance   from   belligerence

                      hard edges worn
            s o f t
      with whiskey and a father's pride
     an international
                    prize-winning daughter
  she

        couldn't remember
her own poison

that night
          only

his acceptance

if he reminds
her at all of her
               father
it is only
     because

when drunk
     he never grows
belligerent or ugly
     he is consistently gracious
(if not fey) he is what her father

was not

        Freudian Fruits de Mer Mélange à la Japonais

two ounces Moonlight Shyochu
two small raw oysters (freshly shucked, Kumamoto
preferred)
one Japanese sweet green pepper
dash of hot sauce

shake shyochu with ice in martini shaker
pour out into discreet
                    tumbler
   slip oysters into
glass, stir
        with the green pepper leave
in glass as garnish
           dash of hot
sauce
(chew the oysters
                  s l o w l y)

D   twenty

after autobiography
the painful stitching together
rank coats worn in the   "world's eye"

will   they embroider shawls, gowns
           cowboy gear, kimonos
           fringed with beads of sweat

born of   one glass   too many

in hours before daylight
sheets besotted by
the fleshy pestilence of living   to its fullest
life

or   do they dance in parental shadows

wilted   blooming
          genes and memories

      imbibing softly
      frequent respites through

indulgence crafting memory into cocktail recipes
concocted boozy fragments
printed on beloved paper placemats
that adorned the Hi Tops, Lychee Palace

Jimmy's   Oriental   Garden

graced by lotus blossom lamps and sparkled green
upholstery on banquettes set for egg rolls alongside
fortunes

you will lead a happy life

H   twentyone

like all the drunks' self
       indulgent reminiscences
nestling sentiment
                    just one more!
  how can they stand

                themselves

when the floor is heaving
when love
turns to self
            loathing

the blur between
trans
     formative personal histories
and performance

             a licensed venue

she and her father drank Zambezi
     beer on the Zambezi
river
     boat tour(ists)
she knew that hippopotami
     (lolling, bobbing, ears atwirl)
could bite you in two

       what did they talk
about that day the water the
turbid emotions below
           the surface
the red dust sun
     in an arid land

she doesn't remember
                              somewhere
there is a journal
in a box
              in a closet she is
not
       going to look

D   twentytwo

the condensation of these ice cubes
in a glass

squat blunt drunken penile objects
bobbing labial petals

on a damp   spent   towel

H   twentythree

condescension
glassy   eyed   wetness

slops over the lip
                      licking the skin
a sticky hand

D   twentyfour

concentration

on internal swizzles

centrifugal   romance

olive beads   pearl necklace   toys

folds and crevices filled

glasses emptied   cups and
bells held in palms   precious bodily gifts
                                       confabulate

kiss   confer   chat   creating   memory

gasp   sigh   suppose
            past events   culminate

in belief patterns   fictitious   truths

covering gaps   volcanic mounds of   flesh

with lips and
         throaty tongue-tied   twisted tendrils

deeply   honest   lies

H   twentyfive

content with
                              forty percent
   titrate nostalgia with
                                        bitter
better
       ahhhhhhh   we are

amusement   per   forming our
selves anointed with fervour and pathos
bushes burning   succour this

                                        need

sucking the pimento
           from the olive
                         rimming the hole

salty clichés
clashing with another
                              asshole
who spilled red wine
(whiner) loved and hated
                              in equal parts

she has never
                   gone home with a stranger

drunk

                 accept
   her
                              self

D   twentysix

pupils   dilate
pimentos hatch

lips
tongue
cock
catch   strung   snails
beach   baubles   frolic gaily

after class

they swam the butterfly stroke   in their
underwear

all the way from

Kaohsiung to China

drank Bombay gin in Beijing
called themselves Darla and Zazu

snatching minnows by a temple

(childhoods captured by insobriety)

     remembering how to   play

                           in sand and water

H   twentyseven

when she read
                    four drinks

considered
              binge drinking she laughed

one ounce or
                         too
much   never quite
                                        enough
(hiding behind two doubles)

all you need
                    of your liver

a quarter
                living
well enough   her oto-san
mourned the books
                              he would never read
so many
                he ordered them   no one

saying the obvious
                              i love you

i love you
              you're such an asshole

(they swam so fast
         they left
a wake
         long into the night)

D   twentyeight

five letters, three words   [i-luv-u]
repeated once, then again
spilling syllables   [i-luv-u]

from misspelled neophyte mouths
salivary glands enfold

thin-lipped smiles entrance
fascinated shyness cups
dazed evening couplets

ear lobe like dew drops flapping
in her tongue's roughened embrace

biting into fear
quivering out of lusty
wayward fantasies

they love each other dearly
through this deconstructed gaze

time travels lightly
crashing along through fluted
stemware meant for toasts

fearlessly drinking into
the truth of fervent friendship

days   roses

      wine

                  of

H   twentynine

one sip
to
        glance
three hard hits
              a deep throat
punch
        and such aglow
oh
        warmwarm the heat
grows
        a flush
flesh needing a thirst
first another one more
fearless travellers
             "in the mood for"
             "all you need is"
                              open
mouthed
left
           wanting

consummate   drinkers

at the Japanese Italian restaurant in Taiwan
she told him about Japanese
animated porn knowing
his predilection for Betty
Rubble (her squeaky sex
noises)
        Po-ru-no, she katakana-ed,
for him
        Pohhh-lllllu nohhhh, he trilled, operatic
magnificence

   and she fell
       off her chair laughing
weeping her joy
you sound like you're ordering
meat in an Italian
deli!
   another! molto bene!

a license to joy
     if only for one moment
something dirty
for my friend

D   thirty

two jade marketeers
scouring vendors' table wares
leaping into trade

soft dense green pupils wander
into retinal focus

brown creamy flesh tones
against delicate sinew
of jaded buyers

involved in firm smooth pendants
inside taut heaving pendants

inside pendants

inside

H   thirtyone

don't buy jade
at the jade market
the taxi driver warned
as a school
of scooters
              swelled
around them
darting minnows in
the undertow
              of smog
eyes wide
with a kind
of longing they nodded hands
reaching for the door (for wallets)
out already
all ready meet you in an hour
as they sampled the wares
                                    alone
beware the taxi driver's words
                                    elicit delicious
they were goblins
long before
              they arrived

D thirtytwo

their last restraint gone
dysphoric maids, ducklings, swans
shopping for trinkets

eroticized ware
she finds demure figurines
he covets her prize

helping him unearth
other beloved objects
consumerist maze

they stumble upon
two miniature lusty maidens
carved from wooden blocks

brazen breasts forward
dangling lantern-ly like orbs
to be held by palms

outstretched fondling flesh
aureoles touch finger
tips by caressing

gently into joy
geisha-like as kimono
slides back revealing pertness

open fan in back
disrobing miniatures
revealing a frog

who climbs the edge of
a simple bathing vessel
toward her buttocks

cupping her sleek hand
as she pulls her right buttock
into bathing pose

these are the objects
representational ploys
of play and pleasure

two bodies simply
posed depicting histories
thru' bounty and joy

bodily excess
come to share heavenly pores
seeking pores seeking

sweat bent rain drops falling
from mouth to mouth to mouth to

full frontal Fireside martinis
1 oz Bailey's Irish Cream
1 oz Japanese Vodka
1 oz crème de cacao menthe

chase around hotel room
with scotch
disrobe   drink   play

H   thirtythree

dishabille me she says

D   thirtyfour

undressed eyes dotting eyes

H   thirtyfive

my cup thirsts

D   thirtysix

crossing t's crossing thighs

H   thirtyseven

unfold   disrobe   suppose

D   thirtyeight

1 oz per cup   undo clasp   behold

H thirtynine

clasping   open   mouthed   mouthing

D forty

undulate wave wrinkle furrow crinkle flutter

H   fortyone

slow, slow,   slow to utter   ly

D   fortytwo

smooth moist skin

H   fortythree

hasten in

D   fortyfour

webbed fingering   feet

H   fortyfive

grazing the lips tonguing   the sweet

D   fortysix

slick tailless toe'd amphibians   lick

H   fortyseven

slipping in   the pond   shadows

D   fortyeight

long back legs slacken   leaping jumping

H   fortynine

glide, glide, water slides

D   fifty

slip   phallo-vagi-centric green machines poised

H   fiftyone

left wanting
                              wanting
   the thirst   thirsts

D   fiftytwo

conceiving conception
                              careful childless
inter-play-fulsome-ness

slake   quench sate   fill

H   fiftythree

slipping out
in dishabille
                                                          she
                                                        he

              all the plenty
aplenty

sating the market
needing the want
left wanting

                      they left
wared, unwary
                              for a drink

D   fiftyfour

slim tall horned glasses
long cool sallies forth

mermaids perched on rims
awaiting intrusive toads
bulbous balloon-like

1 oz orange crush fizzing
1 lime rind curled frond-like

2 oz Chopin vodka
played on the strings
of heart-soaked puree

blend   grin

                    cower

pour

H   fiftyfive

too easy in
the funnel begins
high-end gin   Q

D   fiftysix

martini madness in a hotel lobby bar
red eyes on a red eye
Taipei Vancouver Toronto

landing sober   as if   to say

enough

is   never   enough

H   fiftyseven

altitude not
                    attitude for $5
dollhouse bottles for dollhouse
livers loving
                  lovers living
no
      lies

D   fiftyeight

past captives present poets future tense
anxiety rifled through from rage to page

drawers closets liquor cabinets stowing beer in
bigger breadboxes

empty mickeys   under the rafters

bottled emotional surrender   two

four   the   road

home again home again fly away home
lush live ladybugs descending into respective

local thrones

he went   from
coast to coast
                      from
host to host
                      from
toast to toast

unable to   decide   on proper couplets
to   describe   his corn fed
                          wayward pose

found himself

                 defined as
someone   people helped

73

a maid in waiting   poodle-like   small & docile
prone to fits of silent barking   nail bitten
bridesmaid stripped bare

thinking, paraphrasing country lyrics

    "you didn't leave me sweetheart
    you just beat me to the door"

and as a lad he said to busty strangers

think of my body as   a boundary
                                  a border

don't cross it without care, credentials in hand
don't get too close without a sense
of these terrifying times

be my love
don handsome Customs Official
uniforms from other nations
take me into the custody of your beautiful othered arms

stamp my heart with
privileged white entry
into foreign territory

remember me   as someone
you could   never

quite   grasp

H   fiftynine

like a cat
                    returning
the security of her own
toilet   bowl
cupping her face
                         a porcelain
halo   a seismic con
vulsion re
staining the pure waters
         arching her back curving
w/retched she laughs
         between retching
cottage cheese bits
         sour and vile

bile is the night

D   sixty

no toads to slake the anal thirst
of backsides facing heaven

they find class comfort in their berth like cabins
spewing gut-wrenched warriors

cursing one too many
mornings after glory

banal anal puckers
from end to end

beginnings into middles
into starts both false and true

1 pint beer
3oz clamato juice   stir

spice (to taste)   wrench

                                            slur   sleep
     (celery)
                                            swallow

     (salt rim)

gargle   wash   rinse   repeat

                                                          sleep
slither

                                                  dream

H   sixtyone

water like salt
rising she prays
no more, please
lordjesusipromiseiwon'tdrinklikethisanymore
if that was the last—
bile, bile, the bilge
sluicing the hatch
she bolts
    (so cold)
twists the faucet
    (so cold)
sound rushes like reeds
    clutching her life
preserver she retches like
her father
    being birthed
from her maw
        gagging
retching retching retching no more
    nothing left
she retches yellow
acid sour burns
    hehhhhghuuuu hehhhghuuu hehhhgghuuuuu
her grey stomach
        inside out
ballooning from her mouth
resting
    in a splattered porcelain bowl

D   sixtytwo

discovering solace on the soothing
cool comfort of a tiled floor
bloated ivory porcine pedestal
supports beautiful sinking bellies
hairless, daunting
staring up into eyes
of so many bathroom floors
so many sex-starved strangers
he quantified the quality of mercy fucking
made this his art of loving

unstrained, discovering straight men
who knew, between thin aquiline borders of lust and
particular proclivities

could lie a land of plenty

nausea and self-loathing already sold in street
markets wholesale staring into faces of countless
disenfranchised souls, so what's another drink?
when the alternative is clean living
in a filthy world

close the toilet seat
or your fortune drains away
green petals swirling

                              2 oz cold dark tea
               1 1/2 oz vodka
                        lemon to taste
a spoonful of sugar

                helps

H   sixtythree

Calgary Oviedo
Tokyo Calgary
Calgary Leiden
Nicosia Calgary
Calgary Osnabrueck
         Burnaby   maybe
she thinks
she is wiser (now)
in her fortieth
                        year's time to turn
the page shut
the lid wipe
the bile   from her lips
the back of a trembling
hand

                    love

D   sixtyfour

cities multiply
waking to dysphoric cries
where on earth am I?

seeing familiar skylines
if this is home what was that?

the years of searching
through tall cool glasses
hell-bent hedonists

rising to moments filled with
unadulterated joys

evening drawing in
charismatic shadows fall
patterns forming

questions waiting to be asked
one last fury in the night

H   sixtyfive

the first sip of my
dirty gin three ice cubes full
working friday class

D   sixtysix

wandering homeward
friday night contentment with
one and a half pints

meeting friends on street by chance
two martinis down the hatch

even best laid plans
succumb to heartfelt fondness
for that special glow

a love that dare not mumble
names of beloved boozehounds

monogrammatic
like the grainy wheatened sands
inscribed in wind

>who has seen the boozy breeze
>whisper blithely into dearth

H   sixtyseven

sipping her night
email she writes
him her glass
atop papers
to be filed

a season succumbed
to rain

she misses him

the blue bottle
empty the genie
swallowed three wishes
all there's left
is google

D   sixtyeight

cyberspace intrudes
separated by air waves
boozing never dies

faint heartfelt tremors
missing each other can mean
your aim was never   so great

but their aim was always true
coastlines, mountains, prairies, lakes

a slim low arc of distance
pen pals posed in parallel

two thousand seven hundred forty two vested miles
exiled by divided states

by pigment, gender, sex and
one hundred per cent bulletproof shotgun tin lives

the sveldt hungered droop
jawlines tasting a brazen
detoxified gaze

H   sixtynine

GOTO – Toranobu "Tiger" 1938 – 2005

Cherished husband, exuberant father and grandfather and a generous friend, Tiger passed away quietly at home, at 2:55 AM, on November 22nd, surrounded by the love of his family and friends.

cancer itself doesn't kill
you die from organ failure
the stomach inert
intestines no longer
passing the bowels
blocked the scarred and riddled
liver filters nothing
poisons
remain water re-tension
the cells full to burst
                                  weeping
the skin weeps
the liquid beads on the surface
she watched one form
a perfect droplet
clear and pure
on his taut and swollen leg
it looked so clean
she wiped her forefinger
across the wetness
and brought it to her face
odourless she wondered
Don't taste it! he said
before she finished her
thought how did you know,
she asked
                    it's dirty, he replied

the skin weeps and weeps
leaking what can't
be passed the body
is a miracle
                                        until it's not
a cell divides and grows
a cell divides and grows
a cell divides and grows
a cell divides and grows
a cell detaches and
s t r e a m s down a
                            capillary of blood to
                                  divide and grow
                                  cell divides
                                  grow

he came home
to die

when he lost
consciousness his
breathing slowly
decreasing pattern
"cheyne stoking"
it's called "chain smoking"
she thought (tho liquor's quicker)
she placed her finger
in one perfect bead
forming liquid
on his skin

the taste of tears
on her tongue

D   seventy

candy-like, porous gleaming
Rosacea day-long lollipops
proboscis sugary canes

naming the final moments of a life
with child-like signifiers, symbols, all-day suckers
one last lick sniff gaze

daddy slid rapidly and suddenly out of his life
as quickly as it takes for a highball
to become an empty cut-rate tumbler

so many dimestore lives needing to be led
so little rhyme

compact cars simply slip away through accidental ditches
while the body cracks and folds
coronary arteries quicken, falter, race

happy hours ending with the dull sharp thud
of bar room doors
last call   for

blood

H   seventyone

after her father
died her cells
                    mourned

she wondered
                    why cigarette boxes
                    were so adorned lurid
                    photos of decaying
                    teeth and charcoal lungs
                    of fetuses and pregnant
                    mothers and telltale hearts
but
nothing
                    on the bottles, the pretty shades
of blue and green, golden brown,
red wax seals and silver foil
like christmas
every day
            a bit of poison

every day she
sat at her computer
and opened her
                                        inbox

she pressed get mail
she pressed get mail
she pressed get mail
she pressed get mail
she pressed get mail
she pressed get mail
she pressed get mail

but it never
came

she slowly raised the barrel
of the bottle
to her   mouth

D   seventytwo

Rollerball was on
at the downtown cinema
the night his daddy
slid into a snowbank
his youngest child
and a cousin
by his side

two out of three ain't bad
as survival rates go
in a lime green compact
head on impact
with a half ton
on an icy road

James Caan was a bigger attraction
as his friends thrilled to four wheeled antics
pre-rollerblading loving adolescents
while he mourned the end of
his father's life

to be raised by the post-womb escapades
of a sullen boozy soldier, and then deserted
at the end of his teens
primed for a life
of precarious sudden falls
rolling into raucous drunken soliloquies

to be a lush

or not

H   seventythree

my cup or yours
your thirst or mine
she said what's the
difference matters
matter

between synapse and cock
tails emotions puddle
eloquent their hems
            dragging   wet and filthy
        family heirlooms spinning
ceilings rotate like fans

heart thrums fast
        blood takes its course
its toll the bridge that
bell, that knell, that hard
punch

down the throat

when she was twelve she said i won't

be like him
when she was eight it wasn't
so very difficult
to be his son

D   seventyfour

liking father, liking brother, visiting the sins
of sons, his only sibling
walked into ICU that snowy night in January of '76
and a quarter of a century later
told him that their father looked at him and said

"It's really bad, Pete"

and then he died – Harry Vernon Bateman
decorated soldier, 1918-1976

father, husband, brother, drinker, ribald singer
storytelling friend to all

and now, as he faces his own mortality
some unknown distance to carry the knowledge
of inevitability
he smiles, eyes himself in mirrors saying "Oops"
then laughing wildly into sad air
knowing to have come this far
and enjoyed so much
counting blessings like shots lined up on bars

picking poisons
he cherishes the memory of toxic choices
that filled his loins and arteries with pure
acknowledged joy and sharp exultant sensation

his time will come in verses wrought by self-reflexive
collaborative thoughts
shared with a comrade from another world
wrenched with wild smiles, fearful tears
the mixed sage laughter of some pompous brazen image,
idol sacrificial saintly whore

blue drops on cheekbones
Curacao-coloured crying
rain barrels in spring

blue on blue mourning martini:

6 parts Vodka
1 part blue Curacao
1 dash Angostura bitters
cocktail olive

      rim with salted teardrops

            to   taste

H   seventyfive

oh well she shrugs
her blue jinn
bottle   empty
            Bombay dreaming
last night tonight
she drinks an airplane
shot of vodka, the cute miniature
a forgotten party favour
and searches for more

all that remains:
3/4 bottle aquavit in the freezer
1 small bottle of pungent Korean liquor/smells brown as
burdock
1 bottle of Dutch herbal liqueur/tastes like cough syrup

huh she thinks she's not
                            that alcoholic
if she has no inclination
to drink

            what's left

a shot in the dark
(make it a double)

D   seventysix

he walks to the corner of Elm & University
to see the bust and plaque of Mary Pickford
commemorating her success as the first
internationally acclaimed motion picture star
America's Sweetheart born and raised on a Canadian
cowpath in the midst of
what has become
a lavish boulevard of embassies five star hotels bald bespoken dreams
lined by mammoth hospitals

he crosses four busy lanes
to climb the escalated slopes of Mt. Sinai
waiting eleven months for a psychotherapist
who will tell him everything he already knows
about everything he was not afraid to ask

finding strength in storytelling
the grand reiteration of
all that has come before
in modest chairs replacing
the iconic couches of some Freudian legacy

these cubicles, these makeshift
therapeutic rehearsal halls
for heights still waiting to be scaled

where is she lurking in this dream?

this labyrinthine grimy urban trek
through streets and corridors

in his heart   he tells   himself
as he resists his next tumbler of scotch
wait until late afternoon
after psychotherapy and the long slow
thirst for someone he doesn't know
who will intently listen
to his silent cinematic gestures
moving into talkies

Polyanna narratives
coquettish award-winning performances
He & Mary wrought on corners
    dreams
    boulevards
    lined by

rehab centres

Sick Kids wards   mountains

    he never
meant to

        c
       l
         i
           m
             b

H   seventyseven

drink she said
                    knowing
he would
two mason jars
3/4 full bright red
             strawberry kool-aid
             squeezed lemon
             ice clattering
                         vodka

 one sip
    two gulp
        with each swallow
                      recedes

years fall
away like layers like
skin a veneer a
    worn costume
            a film scrolling backwards
        a flicker of moments
      memory's labyrinth
  unreeling
the heartbreaks
    the sex
the drinking
    loving words
like undergraduates
    of life
  and deathdrinkingdeath
      and every waking breath
          (oh happy avatar
        how lovely thou art)
     forms one act plays
   tragi-comic monologues
flicker past

      staccato of stills
         nothing still
           until
        the jar is empty

      and they stand
hands sticky, lips wet

                            like
                        children how
                        pretty

his soft whiteblonde hair she thinks
how serious her dark brown eyes he thinks

wearing tie-dyed t-shirts and shorts
her sneakers are scuffed, knees dirty
and he is neatly
turned out
        his pageboy
        to her Cleopatra

              i thought i recognized you she mumbles
embarrassed
        a kinship past skin beyond trauma and words
unuttered, histories shared and not and all
        that would otherwise divide
        compromise
                      she doesn't give a shit
            anymore

remember
how to play he asks

she slips
her nail-bitten hand
into his

D seventyeight

taking her hand
he self indulges
building little worlds
on sills, in finely turned dark wooden bowls
sentimental china spoon holders
crystal sherbet dishes
with pedestals like low graduated slopes
of sensible shoes for walks across
these miniature planets
tiny places to stow beloved objects
ideas of order borrowed from some other poet

beloved brazen Geishas from the jade market
shells from the shores of Cyprus
rocks and stones unconsciously tossed together
from all these seas

a small upholstered box
from San Francisco's Chinatown
for some of his mother's ashes
sprinkled effortlessly into mountain wind
flying in his face
over bridges along the edge of hedges
lining homes across the Hollywood Hills
into ashtrays in the Castro

it seemed appropriate
to his sarcastic wizened ways of loving

she was a heavy smoker

all the places they might have gone to play
as he travels alone she still has the power
to force her breadth and beauty into his grin and grimace
with one
false turn of the wrist and elbow as he tries
to free them from each other

but those ashes stick and soil
as he plants them on the earth to sink or foil

he will come and go
the Pieta always struck him
as a reasonable likeness of their lives together
trying to curtail clichés

and failing as the second child
in that constructed familial unit

"he should have been a girl"

not wanting to disappoint
did everything he could to feminize
his time among them
less like Jesus, more like Mary

wandering into temples
donning veils and hats
imagining immaculate conception
some avant-garde drag performance
with a string of Barbies
emerging from between his pubic sequined billowed groin

feather boa-ed fuck fest of
a life in doll-like stages

so she was Ken
his unlikely hero
as they travelled out of regimented verses
into free-wheeling prose

some auto-artificial narrative meant to
soil and sweeten
all these embroidered memories
with the day to day stigmata
of these palms
limp wrists and hands

that vulva
this penis
diving into
un-pre-scripted places

"he should have been a girl"

did everything he could
until they met
plunging headlong

among unexpected lexicons

          of drinking, death

              and glory

H   seventynine

post script
                    magic exists
between memory
and what's recounted
in the embroidery of something
pretty
                    around a cutting edge
she loves
he loves

this is a happy
ending

D   eighty

p.s.

the train sped by last night
he thought of other lovers' houses
by the tracks
how he would run and wave
when rails rattled
rustling poplars rumbled
whistles blew

wind   vivid

passing in the night
packages of sweet and sour
memories to seed

in word, in deed

this is a happy
ending

H   eightyone

condensation beads
on anticipation (the last
sunny day in october)

her sour to his
sweet her
savour to his
cheek
                      don't forget
(don't forget)

D   eightytwo

remembering loss
retrieving joy   post trauma
revisiting doom

leaves   into   gutters
splashes of lime yellow red

russet orange green
long sloe gin-like lapse   into
seasonal   serendipity

colours fall all winter long
summer springing out of love

natural gifts for
writing useful discov'ries
accidentally

cordial-ly invited
into collaboration   trust

H   eightythree

she would
never drink
                    lime cordial
except

with him she would

Perfectly Courteous Martini

2 oz Q gin
1 dash Angostura bitters
a splash of lime
                    cordial

shake tastefully
          pour into frosted martini glass
drop
          a cube of sugar
if you need
                    the sweet

D   eightyfour

he identified with feminized canine figures and sweet citric substances

Lime Cordial Interlude: definitional martini in two parts

1/
Lime: birdlime, sticky substance
       to catch small birds

Cordial: friendly   affectionate
                    sincere   profound
                    stimulating invigorating
      medicinal   alcoholic   drink

            usually   served
                   at the end   of a meal

Poodle: dog with thick curly coat
                          clipped short

developed for hunting   water   retrieval
clipping   facilitating swimming
hindquarters shaved
rosettes of hair   hips & hocks
leaving bracelets of   hair near
feet   & face

pom-pom   at the   tail end   of the

hind

2/
Sticky Poodle Martini:

2 oz lemon gin
2 chunx ice

2 chunx lime
rim glass with honey
1 oz lime cordial

H   eightyfive

a small bird
held
in the mouth

                                          swallow

a boy poodle
nuzzles
his crotch

                                            wallow

D   eightysix

a large heart
melts
into pieces   separating

pomegranate

seeds like
thousands
of hearts   breaking

1 oz green apple Absolut
2 oz champagne
1 tablespoon frozen pomegranate seeds

purse lips   sip   force smile

                              sigh

H   eightyseven

bitterness near the core
seed the heart's translucence
red
              ready
or not
      (you fool)

all the cynics
were once   romantics
yesterday one drink
a way
              home

as epics and tragic narratives
rise and fall around them
the flotsam and jetsam of sound
poets crash like pebbles and
glass and falling branches
they walk across
water without spilling
                    a drop

D   eightyeight

when your greatest fear is spilling your drink
all else pales
beside the comfort of cool calculation

cacophonies   of splash and tumble
tiny broken worlds   of stems and bowls
the inert swirling majesty   of one too many

his wrist and palm becoming foundations for some
12 step planetary programs formed
from stratospheric peer pressure

slim pistils wasted
groups of fused carpels
he raises his glass to toast a blossoming bewildered
pose among
the restrictive gendered carcass

of a flower dying   toy dogs   prancing into mayhem
craving
                                 best in show

depriving divas   slow   dancing
slouching   thirsting
                                         bent

H   eightynine

gently gender go softly into the nightclub tailing cocks
and mocking muffs sweet

D   ninety

Caucasian circles in the sand pebbles grainy
fore-skinned presence marking time's wash

H   ninetyone

hot toddies dash sashay loosing chagrin
a grin gin come in

D   ninteytwo

dashing past destined rendezvous inscribed on icy
fingertips

H   ninetythree

another round speaks elide memories membrane
she and he

D   ninetyfour

wolves dancing mindlessly conscious of the hollow grin

H   ninetyfive

baring hides skin teeth howling last call

D   ninetysix

for alcohol: pear vodka, clearly shaken

H   ninetyseven

fear not heart kiss me

D   ninetyeight

and then they kissed

David Bateman is a spoken word poet and performance artist presently based in Toronto. His most recent performances, *A Brief History of White Virgins* or *The Night Freddy Kissed Me*, and *What's It Like?* were presented in Vancouver, Peterborough, Ottawa, Montreal, and Toronto during the winter of 2009. He has presented his work across the country over the past twenty years and also teaches drama, literature, and creative writing at a variety of Canadian post-secondary institutions. His performance work has been published by Blizzard Press, Ordinary Press, and finewords chapbooks.

Hiromi Goto is the award-winning author of *Chorus of Mushrooms*, and *The Kappa Child*. She has also written a children's novel, *The Water of Possibility*, and a collection of short stories, *Hopeful Monsters*. Her most recent publication is a young adult novel, *Half World*, published by Penguin Canada. She and David Bateman collaborated on and showcased a performance piece entitled *The Cowboy and the Geisha*.